BIG WORDS FOR LITTLE PEOPLE

Helen Mortimer & Cristina Trapanese

Calmness

Kane Miller
A DIVISION OF EDC PUBLISHING

Quiet

Sometimes all we need to be calm is a quiet place.

Sssshhh!

Feel safe

Our friends support and protect us. We can share a safe space where we can all feel calm.

Breathe

When you breathe in deeply and breathe out gently it soothes your body.

Don't worry

Worries can get in the way of staying calm so it's important not to hide them away.

I'm a bit worried.

What about?

Talk about the things that make you feel anxious—as a way to let them go.

Focus

When you focus on the things you love to do instead of your worries, you will feel more relaxed.

You could lose yourself in a book, draw
a picture, or let music fill you up.

Time

Something as simple as walking gives you time to watch and listen while you move.

Pause

Sometimes it's important to stop for
a moment. Think about how it feels
when you close your eyes and slowly
count to four . . .

Two

One

Three

Four

Imagine

. . . or just imagine something peaceful!

Jump, push, or squeeze

If you are not feeling calm, you can jump, push, or squeeze things to get past your angry feelings.

Balance

Busy times are best balanced with moments of staying still.

Softly, softly

When you speak softly and listen closely
to your friends, it helps everyone to
share a sense of calmness.

Calmness

Calmness can be all around us.

Find calm places. Think calm thoughts.

Ten ideas for getting the most from this book

1 Take your time. Sharing a book gives you a precious chance to experience something together and provides so many things to talk about.

2 Read slowly, calmly, and quietly, and enjoy how it makes you feel.

3 Talk about the things that make you feel calm.

4 This is also a book about language. Ask each other what words you would use to describe being calm.

5 The illustrations in this book capture various moments in an outdoor space. The illustrator has used lots of calming blues and greens. Do you have a favorite color for making you feel calm?

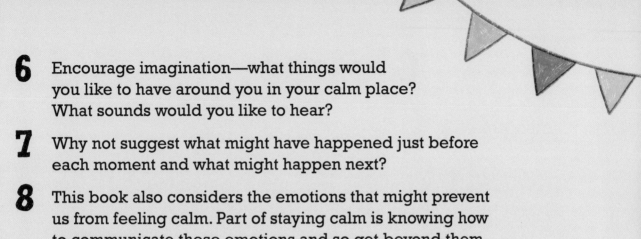

6 Encourage imagination—what things would you like to have around you in your calm place? What sounds would you like to hear?

7 Why not suggest what might have happened just before each moment and what might happen next?

8 This book also considers the emotions that might prevent us from feeling calm. Part of staying calm is knowing how to communicate these emotions and so get beyond them more easily.

9 By exploring ways to recognize and express how calmness can have a positive impact on everything we do, we hope this book will give children and the adults in their lives the tools they need to make sense of themselves and the world around them.

10 You could each choose a favorite word about calmness from the book—it will probably be different each time you share the story!

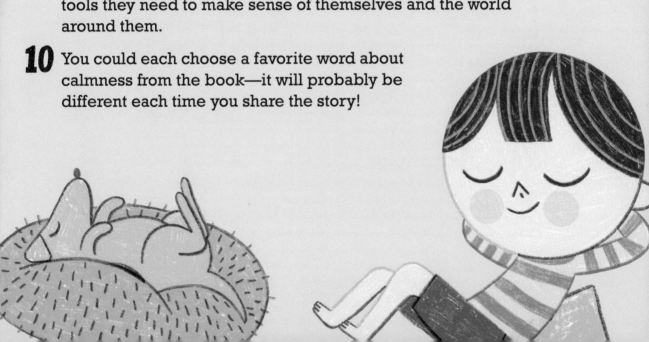

Glossary

anxious – if we are anxious, we feel worried

lose yourself – if you lose yourself in something,
    you forget about everything else around you

softly – quietly and gently

soothe – something which soothes us makes
    us feel relaxed and happy

support – when you support someone,
    you help them